T0158697

ALSO BY LINDA HUSSA

POETRY

*Where The Wind Lives*
*Ride the Silence*

NON-FICTION

*Diary of a Cow Camp Cook*
*Lige Langston: Sweet Iron*

FORTHCOMING

*Shared Fencelines*

BLOOD SISTER, I AM TO THESE FIELDS

# Blood Sister, I Am To These Fields

*New and Selected Poems*

## LINDA HUSSA

RAINSHADOW EDITIONS
BLACK ROCK PRESS
UNIVERSITY OF NEVADA, RENO
2001

ISBN 1-891033-19-0

The Black Rock Press
University Library/322
University of Nevada, Reno
Reno, NV 89557-0044

www.library.unr.edu/blackrock

Cover illustration by Michael Drury

Poems from:

*Shared Fencelines*
(to be published by the University of Utah, 2001)

*Lige Langston : Sweet Iron*
(University of Oklahoma Press, 1998)

*Ride the Silence*
(Black Rock Press, 1995)

*Where the Wind Lives*
(Gibbs Smith Publisher, 1994)

Manufactured in the United States of America
First Edition

*Dedicated to John, as always*

# CONTENTS

FROM *Ride the Silence*

FROM *Where the Wind Lives*

# Acknowledgments

Grateful acknowledgements to the publishers of *Dry Crik Review*, *Graining the Mare : The Poetry of Ranch Women*, *Maverick Western Verse*, *Between Earth and Sky: Poets of the Cowboy West*, *Cowgirls*, *Cowboy Poetry Matters*, and *Fishtrap Anthologies*. To Gibbs Smith, publisher of *Where the Wind Lives*; the Black Rock Press, publisher of *Ride the Silence*; University of Oklahoma Press, publisher of *Lige Langston : Sweet Iron*; University of Utah Press, publisher of *Shared Fencelines*.

To family and friends who, when I ask, "Have you got a minute?" patiently respond, "Yes." To the sharp eyes and the gentle hearts of Laurie Wagner Buyer and Jerry Martien who let me see a clearer line to the work of writing. To Michael Drury for finding Surprise Valley, for coming back with an eye for its perfection. And, most particularly to Bob Blesse, a dear friend whose vision and design makes this book so beautiful.

*Blood Sister, I Am To These Fields*

# PUT ON YOUR FACE

The desert puts on its face in Spring
when tidings of rain scatter rabbitears,
Indian paintbrush, lupine, wild peach,
pink and purple phlox, primrose.
The feathery bloom of mahogany
carpets thickets into Fall and sage
does its best with the perfume.

My father used to smile at my mother.
      Go put on your face
        and I'll take you to town.

Otherwise, the desert is plain and simple.

# THE APPLE TREE

1.

I ask Mother again and again
the moon, the day of the week of my birth.
She says there is another memory
stronger than the one of birth.

A month before
summer clouds darken the kitchen
and thunder cracks across the back of the house.
(screendoor slams, rain hammers the roof, yard)

She runs to take the wash from the line
(jolt of her heart beating out quick movements,
slip and click of wooden clothespins
dropping in her apron pocket near my head,
whipping leaves of the apple tree above us,
the roiling sky beyond, dark, deep)
her arm gripping laundry and me
when the threads of suspension — give.
(flick of a tadpole in fertile jelly)

Arms clasp beneath her stomach,
she crouches against the tree
(flick again)
her face presses into Father's shirts
blown through with August.
(there was a winter child spilled on ice)

Rain wets her as she leans
into the heave and wrench of roots
waiting for the parting to mend itself.

Her stillness flows through me.
I take up my ripening.

2.

I dial the phone
and when she says hello
I say
  Tell me some good news, Mom.

And she says
  I'll tell you
as good as I've got.

Then her voice skips across the air
hardly touching down on
  biopsy
  test results
  an appointment on Monday
  options.

To help me up
she says
  I do have *some* good news.

But I am still rolled in barbed wire
unable to move
only blink my eyes.
In my silence
she hears the signal for — go ahead


  Remember that little black heifer I bought
  that turned up bred,
  couldn't have weighed 5 and a half —?
  Well, she calved.  We had to help her
  but she had a nice little bull
  and they're doin good.

I loosen the wire wrapped hard on my jaw.

I've got some good news, too Mom.

And then I have to make something up.


3.

I look across the field.
I can't see behind me
but the world is there too.
If I turn to see that distant row of trees
the broken mountain top disappears
cautiously,
and dangerous things
or beautiful things happen
while my attention is on that cow
walking slowly toward the pond.
That must be how God feels
trying to keep track of us all
— all at once.
It explains how the child
follows the ball into the street,
how the doctor — never blinking —
said, "Cancer."

I feel your chill,
though you do not move at all.
What did God do then?


4.

Childhood binds me to the natural world
as planks lashed to logs make a raft.
I pole such a raft from the shore of our small pond.
Breezes chop the water in a blinding pattern
or smooth it so that on my back or stomach
clouds live in sky, in water.

Killdeer dip and bob on the muddy bank
calling out a sound I try to sing.
A white trillium grows beside a path
where our horses cross into the woods.
Three lunar petals
on a thin stem rising from the pine duff.

In the apple tree sturdy enough for a girl to climb
a branch forks where I curl to nap.
I know its rest. I know its flowering.
I learn the swelling skin
beneath the wilted skirts of a blossom
will grow into fruit.
I wait through summer,
tasting the pucker of green fruit,
each day sweeter.
On a certain day
I make a basket of my shirttail
and carry the harvest to my mother.

# Return

After you've gone
I notice your overnight bag
on the bench by the screen door,
shaving kit, freshly ironed shirt.

Anxious to attend the cattle sale,
to sit among other cattlemen
as our calves enter the ring,
and, although there has not been
an angry word between us,
to be away from me for two days.

On the afternoon of your return
I sweep my hair up,
lipstick — *Tender Rogue*,
the perfume — *Il Bacio*, (the kiss).

Chore time comes.
You're not home yet.
I take the ribbon loose,
pull on coat, hat, gloves

pitch hay to the calves.
The dogs hear your truck coming.
They race to meet you
barking and wagging their silly tails.

## Pointillist

I prefer the willow now
in earliest spring
when each new leaf
is a small dot of green

catkins only commas
at the end of each leafy thought.

# On a Clear, Cold Calving Night

Before I leave the human world
and enter the calving shed
of muttering cows
I stop and search bright stars
for Orion
standing astride two worlds.
I've pinned my precious father
on the center star
— the buckle of Orion's belt —
and there he is
as long as I look up and nod.

That he ever lived
seems as improbable
as the possibility of his eternal passage
in brilliant light.
Yet, I am made of his particular laugh
and his serious errors.

I have learned to reach into the sacred womb,
grasp a placid hoof
and coax life toward this certain moment.

If only I could
from the dust of all souls
lost between here
and infinity
draw forth the ones I need.

# Rural Electricity – 1938

When the generator broke down
the men had to milk the cows
by hand.
Sucking cups, hoses useless
as 'tits on a boar,' they snorted.

The scrub board came down
from the attic and leaned haphazard
in the steaming galvanized tub.
Rubber wringers of the washing machine
like a gummin' grandpap
sadly eyeing a cob of corn.

Oh joy!
When the electricity hooked in
on poles set over the low saddle
of the mountains
and the switch was thrown

children ran from room to room
turning on every light
— starry constellations
seen the length of the valley night.

# Accounts Payable

Billy Fenwick sold
a washboard
one day
at the Eagleville store.

But for the life of him
he couldn't remember who to.
So he billed all
his charge customers for
"one washboard".

They all paid.

# Darby Creek

Dedicated to the five-hundred farmers, many of them Amish and Mennonite, being forced from their land on Darby Creek, in Ohio to make room for a wildlife refuge. But not dedicated to the man on the radio who said, "Farmers and ranchers are a dime a dozen."

Who is there to tell us that we do not matter, to say that it does not matter that we were born and lived in the house with the worn white paint and the apple tree in the front yard and went to Sunday School at the grange on the hill where the Golden Rule was written perfectly on the chalk-board above the lesson for the day, and on Friday's Mrs. Lay brought out the stack of blue savings books held with a red rubber band she slipped onto her wrist and called out our names, one by one, and we got up from our chairs and walked quietly up the aisle, reached out our hand taking the book with our name inside from her hand and made our deposit of 5 cents or 10 cents and gave it back to her and she stamped the book with the tiny date and put our money in a bag with a string sewn on to the top? We learned to save. We learned that today was important but tomorrow promised something new and better and the only way to get there was to make weekly deposits and never lose sight of the purpose. Our nickel would stack by others we had saved from turning in orange Nehi bottles at the store or helping with chores or chopping the wood or picking blackberries for the neighbor lady. Someday our money would be enough to take us some place or buy something special for someone special or with enough saving we could—like our parents—buy land and clear a place for a house and build that house and plant a tree for the children to climb and lie on a limb and look far and dream and we could grow a crop to harvest and sell and at evening we could walk out and sit on our hill and know our work and our faith in our work meant something fine was happening in the world. Oh, we would pay a part to bring the school bus out from town so the kids wouldn't have to walk and for the men who filled the pot holes in the road and to keep the firemen in the station for emergencies because we passed the Thompson's house on the way to town and we remember the smell of it burning waking us from sleep and the awful red of the fire in the night sky and now just the chimney is there and even it is ruined. We don't mind saving a bit for those things, taking a bit away from the blue savings book, even though we had to give up a used baler that would make getting the hay in easier and father wouldn't come in so tired; and put off stringing lights to the barn for the times we had to tend cows at night and used the flashlight to find why the calf was not coming right. We thought it was right when land was taken for parks so people could camp and walk in a place unlike the place where they live. And we thought it was right that companies that harvested from the earth should pay a little to do that harvesting and pay a little to make sure no animals were put out or hurt by their work. But now people we have hired to work for us, to keep an eye on things are shaving off, and making laws and restricting and writing violations and levying fines and taking to court and sending to jail and denying rights and denying ownership and denying access and saying it is for the benefit of humankind and my little blue savings book is wrong and Mrs. Lay is wrong and owning is wrong and pride is wrong and freedom has changed and the Golden Rule? I don't know about the Golden Rule. I guess it is wrong too, because I could not take away someone's home or barn or fence kept in good repair or sharp knoll or gravel road or beet field or orchard or cow pasture or garden spot or town or meeting place or school or place they were born or place of their childhood or place they buried their people or place they sat of an evening when chores were done and dishes were washed and mother sat with the children helping them understand that one apple and one apple are two apples and five apples minus four apples leaves one apple or no apples because the apple tree is no longer theirs and they will be moving before harvest so their land can be set aside for wildlife with no roads in and no sounds of people living near and the children ask if it will be like the time before the pilgrims when only animals and Indians lived here and she said not exactly.

# COMET HYAKUTAKE

*March 1996*


So big, this lamb
even though the ewe is past 15
and used to lambing time.
She jams her head against a post
in her despair.
I find her so at mid-night
water flushed, only tips of hooves protruding,
agony in her deep moan.

Weak, flanks trembling,
she lets me push her to a jug.
Once through the gate
she sees the lamp on golden straw
and leaves my hands to stand
within the ring of light cast downward.

I wrap straw around emerging legs
to give me grip and brace my feet
in her curve of hocks. She presses hard
and groans a sound that feels human.
Long minutes pass
before the head pops through.

I drag the lamb to her head.
Her licking bonds them.  He mews
and she — in mother tones — responds.

I wait awhile with this new pair
and from where I sit on straw
watch Hyakutake Comet born
woolly among a host of stars.

## The Old Pair

That crane with the bum leg is back,
he told her as he washed his hands at the sink.
She stood beside him peeling off long leaves of lettuce
and breaking them into her mother's blue bowl.
Her back was to him as he set her pills beside her plate
so he barely heard her ask
Is the female with him?


..


Days went by
and she stopped asking about the cranes.

She folded the frayed edges of the old cotton
and sewed each small piece into the pattern of the quilt.
Julia sat across from her at the frame.

Julia said
Did I tell you how Coyote tried to catch Crane
by climbing to the top of the pine tree
and jumping on her back as she flew by?


..


Her graceful wings reached into the width of the sky,
flowering the dullness of twilight.
She saw him standing in the clear water
by the willows, pulled from the others
and set down nearby.

He threw his head back to let out a purr
of rusty hinges opening.
He honed his beak on hers in greeting
and then they pranced, leaped
capes and coat-tails, fancy fans shaking, forgetting
Fall is not the time for their mating dance.

# House Cats

Paiute boys too young for heavy work on the school farm were kept in the inside quarters and given easier tasks. The older boys nicknamed them "house cats."
— *The Fort Bidwell Indian School, 1898–1940*


Spit soiled thread,
clumsy knots,
a sorry copy
of the teacher's example
you sewed buttons
in the upstairs barracks
and where was your mind?

Older boys worked in the shop's dark file,
ran from the bay of the constable's dogs
into deep winter ice
crossing sloughs and swamps
to sleep or die
in the willow stands.
Older boys — mute if the split leather strap
was taken from the hook,
whispered forbidden Paiute
from their sour bedding
like bats scratching
for a hole to the sky

and the house cats bent over their work
sewing on buttons
— one short thread pulled uneven.

# NATIVE MYTH

In memory of Clarence Degarmo


The Serpent
that lived in this valley
carved a trough along the hills
with his long tail
dropping acid spore
where vents spew steam.

When Lake Surprise drained
down a secret path
he followed it toward Pyramid Lake
and from there — no one knows.

Rain came heavy this winter.
The lake has filled.   I look
for dimples of his oil on the stones
and when it is a dark moon
I listen for heavy dragging
of his black and ivory tail
against the gravel bar.

## BLUE BIRD

He said,
      "There's a Blue Bird
      dead.
      Back there."

We put the cattle through the gate
      and rode back to the place.

It lay over my hand
      a swatch of blue silk
      soft
      warm

      one leg gone
      blood
      ran down my skin.

I fanned the wing and imagined
it disappearing against the sky.

      Would the wind wait on the hill
      and wonder?

# GRANDMA, MOSES

Apples hanging from the lower limbs
are plumb bobs that knock my head
as I mow the grass underneath.
Each thump is Grandma's thimbled finger
rapping my hollow noggin
if I was smarty or answered back
to remind me, "don't forget yourself."

We stopped the night at Grandma's.
Finally, my turn
to sleep in her featherbed.
After my bath Mother knelt, drying my hair,
buttoning the neck of my gown.
"Lie still and don't kick her."

I knew bed etiquette. My sister pounded me
for getting on her half of our bed,
screamed if I touched her.
I laid as still as mashed potatoes,
the feather mattress was gravy up to my chin.

Grandma's house creaked with the moonrise.
Her canary cage hung by the window
draped in a night cloth, ghostlike.
She lay quietly beside me, her long gray braid
still as a snake on the folded blanket top.
Suddenly she spoke into the darkness,
"Where was Moses when the lights went out?"

Oh, no! A bible story question! The price
of sleeping in Grandma's featherbed.
I squinched my eyes tight trying to remember.
Moses parted the water. Moses had an overdue book
at the Mount Sinai Lending Library.
I looked aloft where all answers are written.
The ceiling was blank. I gave. Ashamed I asked,

where was Moses when the lights went out?
"In the dark" Grandma cackled. In the dark.

I decided I would give up my turn
in Grandma's featherbed next time we visited.


I turned the mower and entered the shade.
An apple knocked my head.
Again I felt Grandma's thimble,
"Where was Moses when the lights went out?"
A magpie laughed down from the limb above,
"Down in the cellar eating sauerkraut!"

# 3 R's

He was the boy with the "C" grades
and to this day
doesn't figure himself very darned smart.
He had hell in math class, hog-tied
by formula, theory, logic. Cow camp
lived in his daydreams juſt beyond
the thin, clear window glass

—Horses, ropes, hightimes
not school buses and tardy bells
and Mr. Page's pop-quiz,
not Mom calling him in from the barn
if he forgot to make his bed or
siſter's tight grip on the honor roll,
or Dad's idea of working cattle
(tie your horse to the fence and get a ſtick).

And yet, he can eyeball a pen of cattle
to a whisker point on the rocking scale arm,
figure pounds of seed to the acre,
the tonnage of hay in the field by lifting a bale,
how to balance a load of cattle over the axles,
the carrying capacity of a paſture,
rate-of-gain, intereſt rates, geſtations,
growing seasons, how much hay we need
for winter feed, and whether a lease will pencil-out
— all in his head.

There's something to be said about practical
application and commonsense combined with
the beautiful boogie-woogie of book-learnin'
reflected off the schoolroom window
and the houlihan catch of a boy's brain.

## John's Poem

My Hero? he grinned.
Casey Tibbs!
From the time I
was in high school.
Nineteen,
world champion bronc rider,
silk shirts,
purple Caddy, pretty women
on
his
arm, and

I
wanted to be
just like Casey.

Any horse'd fire
I rode it
— or tried to.

Mom
listened to me
croon his name,
as I shaped my new black hat
with Casey's crease
in the steam of her tea kettle.

She pulled a newspaper clipping
from her apron pocket
slapped it down
and tapped the headline
— wind warnings in her eyes:
CASEY — NAMED IN PATERNITY SUIT

That was as close
to sex education
as we ever got
in our house.

# His Cowgirl Rides the Copper Horse

Horse heads hung sleepy
over stall doors in the narrow alley of the barn.
She perched on the horseshoe keg.
He leaned on the anvil. They talked
high school rodeo, decided bits, training,
how to rope calves fast.

Time came she rode away to college,
work, marriage, baby. They talked
on the phone - first tooth, and daycare.
Then she bought a horse and rode back home
on the telephone wires.

Three thousand miles apart,
hands in the air, he doubles the colt
or turns it in one swift motion,
then listens.

They talk bits, running martingales,
gooseneck trailers, slick fork saddles.
Bloodlines. Flying changes.

## ORBITS

Sometime after four, I start the coffee
and take the puppies outside - two
border collie pups with nearly
impeccable house manners

trot behind me, nipping my bare legs,
practicing for the day I would be a cow.
There is no moon.

Just yesterday morning
it was a slice of orange someone had eaten
and tossed its peel above Orion's shoulder.

I admire the minds of ancient astrologists
who read stars as heavenly art,
for I would never imagine Orion
standing in the sky. I see belt and sword
but not the flesh that makes a man.

Quiet night. Cows weaned of calves
come up the field to drink sweet water
at the tank and lumber away again. Their milk dries
into bones of another calf growing within.
The eastern rim warms with a late rising moon

and the puppies sit beside me, looking up
as if I am their constellation, huge, mystic,
hard to make out.

I go inside, pour the coffee and carry a cup
to my man. Warm with sleep, he turns
in the blankets and draws the sheet aside.

In the morning sky that arc of light
lifted, aglow with sun's heat
all but blocked by earth.

## SEVEN CATS IN ICE

Below zero dawn
on my kitchen window sill
seven barn cats
wait.

Some sit upright
others tuck front paws
underneath, tails curled
to chink the space between.

Humped, rounded bodies
and sharp ears
melt swirls and whorls
in jackfrost.

In the sudden glare of sun on glass
steam rises around them.

When they jump down
seven cat-shapes remain
— edges dripping
like candlewax.

## SURRENDER

**1.**

Fall came while we were away
as if painters had brightened
the worn clapboard siding
with touches of scarlet Virginia Creeper
and Weeping Birch.
Along the creek -here and there –
a branch in the willows has given up,
sending flame through dull green.

**2.**

He fell coming home from Senior Center,
didn't want to worry us on the phone,
doesn't know how long he lay on the path.

I bring hearty beef soup with carrots
from the garden he tended all summer,
hoed awhile, then rested

on a chair under the plum tree
as each lettuce leaf unfurled, each blossom
became crookneck, potato, melon.

He pauses as he lifts his spoon
and says nearly inaudibly,
if I pass away ...

**3.**

We spread vacation photographs
— rafts on the Colorado
bright against red rock cliffs,
green water churning, or placid.

Each frame is a double exposure.
Fixed in our brains' emulsion
he tries to get to his feet,
grasping the trunk of the young pear,
its limbs reaching straight up, beseeching.

*Shared Fencelines*

# Oat Crop

Stub pencil on the fender
the old man figured the seed —
eighty pounds to the acre
— all his last year's grain crop
harvested, sacked, stored in the tin granary,
to plant this 60 acre corner field.
It was a cold spring – that last one - and dry to boot.
Lucky to turn off at all.

Now that he's dead, I'll be using his old drill.
The green paint rusted through clean down to the iron,
converted in the '30's from a team of horses.
I hook it to our wheel tractor I call Trigger
because it rears up when I start off.

Top-off the gas, check the oil, radiator,
service the drill, grease all the zerts,
every moving part, check each feed funnel
and set the gauge to trickle down oats onebyone
onto the seed bed ahead of the packers.

Every sack I leg, belly, arm wrestle, grunt
up to the drill box, and fight
the sacker's knot. Finally, it ripcords,
spilling hard, blond seed with a whoosh,
slippery good, even over the holes.
I pluck up a single oat, roll it
on my tongue, soak it in my juice,
bite down for luck, toss it in the box.
Oats that came out of this ground
are oats going back in today.

Trigger's iron seat's already butt blistering hot.
I kick it into gear, eyeball a straight line
to a fence post or gulley or sagebrush
the way a sailor sets course by a certain star.

Trigger rears up.  I spur him a lick
and go steady all dayandtomorrowandtomorrow
back, forth. At the row end,
I stand on the inside brake, lock the wheel.
Trigger comes hard around compass-wise
combing an empty loop in the dirt
that will drill out on the final round.

I cherish those flaxen oats laid out
under this pieced pattern of loam and clay
to thread toward the sun, sweetening,
ripen past milk to soft dough,
nod heavy in the wind,
to multiply itself by twenty
— unless it turns off dry or cold
or early rain rots the seed.
But we can't *not* try. Hell!
It's mostly luck anyway — all of it.

I wear the sun in my eyes and I will sleep with its light.
I eat the dust and feel its weight in my bones.
Hours fall behind me like these rows.
I stop to fill the drill box again and again.
School bus comes down the lane.
Little sprouts packing lunch buckets and color
books get off and play their way home.
Bus turns around, goes back for the big ones.

Early spring I prepared the ground,
combed out the tangles. Today I plant the seed.
I'll tend it just as the old man did,
watch the field come up through summer,
hip-high, dollar bill green. When the oats ripen
we'll pull the combine into the field.
The reel will gather to it, the shaker
will pass the seed along to fill the sacks
row for row.

A measure to feed the stock when snow lays on.
A measure saved back for next year's seed.
A measure to mark my passing over the land.

Blood sister, I am to these fields.

# The Neighbor

1. The Handshake

The dogs didn't even bark
when he drove into our front yard,
struggled from behind the steering wheel.

*Standing up he's stooped,*
*ready to step under the low cellar door.*
*His is always a view of the long horizon.*
*I wonder if he remembers how it was*
*to look up at the sky.*

He asks if we would like to buy
his cattle. They're just too much work.
We've seen them, he says.

*We've seen them all right. Every morning*
*hay is scattered in the stack yard,*
*phantom tracks meander through the flowerbed,*
*under our bedroom window.*

They've been busting out, he says. Gettin' breechy.
Nothing he hates worse.

*His lane fence is completely gone in places.*
*A pallet or odd board dangles from wire*
*strung to rose briars. He cobbles it up*
*when someone calls to complain.*

All of the cows are bred up, he says.
Some spring calvers but the rest
have big calves on 'em.

*They're bred up, all right, by a gang*
*of two-year-old bull calves he didn't get cut.*
*His bloodlines have thickened considerably.*

John says we'd only be interested in the open heifers.
The two men shake hands on the deal.

*I catch myself straightening my back*
*and looking up at the plain blue sky.*


2. The Profit

Mr. Jones made his best deal
and turns his truck around in our yard.

At home he tells the wife, They bought the heifers.
We'll weigh them Wednesday. They smile,
nodding at each other, satisfied.

He goes out again before dark, starts the tractor
and with a bale of lush alfalfa dribbled from the wagon,
leads his cattle in from grass.
In his stooped way he separates the heifers off
and looks them over. Eight head straight English.
The price was under market.

He forgot he pays no freight, no sale yard
commission, no beef promotion, no brand inspection.
As my father would say, "He can't stand prosperity."

He chums the eight fat heifers into a smaller corral
closer to the barn door. Thick flakes of green alfalfa
stagger across the lot. They rip off mouthfuls,
eyes shut on this lovely new taste, lips painted green.
He drops a block of salt beside the water tank,
spanks his hands together
and goes in to his own supper.

Dawn slips across his field, stutters,
nudges at two heifers grotesque in death,
bloated like poisoned pups
on the neighbor's need.

3. The Lesson

Mr. Jones says don't worry about paying
for the six heifers until the Fall.
He won't need the money until then.
We won't brand the heifers until we pay for them, John says.

He asks if we want to run any cows with his
since we're taking the heifers.

We'd have to put a bull with them, John says,
to get them bred up.

That's all right, he says.

This year, he has no herd bull for his cows.

He doesn't know how he's going to get his calves branded.
There's just Mrs. Jones and him now.

At first light we drive his cattle to our corral.
His are hen-skin thin in some places. We brand,
castrate the bull calves, vaccinate, the works.
Drive them back home.


(Summer seeds harden into yellow fat. Frost
lies down on the backs of the heifers.
They are young cows now, sprung in the flank,
bred up to calve in the spring.)

The neighbor drives into the front yard.
He says since he has a lot of feed left.
And the price has come up.
He has decided not to sell the heifers, after all.
We can bring them home.
And move our cows and bull anytime.
We watch him drive out. I look at John,
not sure what he'll say.

He breaks into laughter.
We sit down on the grass and laugh.
We lay back on the grass, still laughing.
We hug each other and laugh and then we just hug
and watch a small bunch of specks flying south
over the bank of black willows.


4.

Night never leaves his windows.
Mornings are cold. They are hungry for meat.

Mr. Jones drives into our yard and waits in his car.
John puts his sandwich down and goes out without his hat.

His forehead is Irish white. His cheeks and throat
are browned with summer. His dark hands rest
on the neighbor's door as he says hello.

He asks if John would butcher a steer for him
for half the meat. It's been on grain 90 days.
Should be good. Anytime it's handy. No hurry.

John looks hard into the deal for the loophole
hanging above his head. Seeing none, he agrees.
The next morning before there's a light
in their kitchen window we drive the wall-eyed steer
out of his corral, across his fields to our gate.
By six his steer is hanging on the gambol.
Blood puddles around our boots.

At eight the neighbor drives in,
says when John butchers the steer
 he should cut the oxtail deep
— veed into the haunch —
so there will be plenty of meat for soup.
They're hungry for meat.
It's too late. We've finished butchering his steer.

The beef is in halves, clean and still as the cross beam
it hangs from, the tail cut square.
They must make-do on that or organ meat.

Which half are you going to take, front or hind?
His eyes are steady with the question.

Split 'er down the middle.
We'll each get stew meat and steaks, even-steven.

He nods and looks at the hide
stretched on the fence rails dripping
pinkish water into the dirt.
Rank smelling offal has been hauled downcreek
for scavengers.
The head is skinned out the old way
- cheeks, tongue, floating in icy water
with the liver and heart. The brain
was hacked out of its chamber of pure white bone.

He hobbles toward the skull but the name
he called all summer from the granary gate
burned like bile in his mouth.
He looked into the lidless eyes
and made a hasty sign of crossing
before he turned away.


5.

(At the meat market the butcher asks,
This your beef, John?

No, he says, my neighbor's.
He gave me half for butchering it.
Split 'er down the middle. Even-steven.

We'll let 'er hang awhile, then I'll box it
just that way.)

A month or so later there's snow on the ground.
The neighbor follows the county plow up the road,
into the yard, rolls his window down.
His breath glitters, frozen around him.

John walks out of the shop, a pair of jumper cables
in his hands, on his way to ſtart the feed truck.
The neighbor leans away from John
half-expecting to feel the red cable clamp
on his ear — positive to positive.
An apology slips over the sharp edge of the glass.

Remember when I said, — The woman
went through all the meat and said
she couldn't find any ſteaks, juſt hamburger
and roaſting meat. Hussy muſta got away
with *all* the ſteaks. We got no ſteaks, a'tal?—
Wal, we looked again.
Clear down in the bottom
T-bone, sirloin, chuck, round, New York,
juſt like you said. I'm sorry, John. I hope
you're not mad at me.
He wasn't mad. It was too late
to get mad. And besides
he had a soft spot in his heart
for the crippled old man.

# DOWNSTREAM

In that house across the field
they accommodate God's will
on a blackboard by the back door,
a psalm to start the day or end it,
to accept the portion dealt
from life's unlevel spoon.
Their land is dry
unless the upstream neighbor,
owning first flow rights,
turns water out all winter,
lets his ditches freeze
in wells above the ice,
to hold and hold, to overflow
beyond his fields
where water doesn't know
that fences have a name.
Then his meadows fresh with flood,
the dormant seeds will split the skin,
radicle and cotyledon,
worm down and up to dark and light
— all things making use of both,
the blackboard keeps them mindful of.
The ground will dole out moisture
to satisfy the root, to flesh the leaf,
to fill the sleeve.
A simple man, his needs are just:
pasture for his cows,
a bait of decent food
to feed his rough-cheeked children
gathered 'round the kitchen stove
with books, and toys and handwork.
The rooms are small,
don't ask much wood to heat them.
The pines he planted as a lad
keep snows from shouldering up the walls.
He fills his plate with beef he raised,

picks his teeth with gratitude
for his neighbor's water
that gives him yet another year.

But last winter the upstream neighbor
turned the ditch, let it flood the channel,
let it carry to the lake because he tired
of cleaning out forgotten toys of summer
and paper sacks and weeds
that dammed the culverts, and damned him
when townsfolk drew their miseries
out in one long breath.
He took his share in spring
but not enough to cross the land
and reach the man downstream.
Drought laid on year after year
and no rain fell except in numbers
he could count like stones
across the road.
The meadow parched,
blew off in dust.
The pond cracked open.
Moans of the drought shook
above the ground in waves.
He pumped the house-well
to keep the orchard living.
The towering cottonwoods
around the house
put out leaves like lilac,
small and cupped to gather dew
and by the first of August
reached grey bones of branches
clattering in the winds.
He weaned calves as light as leppies
to save the cows from falling off.
The blackboard was rubbed clean
and in its blankness was the prophet.
The neighbor hoards the sin of ignorance.
The believer lives downstream.

# New Mown Hay

1.
I mow the meadow. I mow the timothy. I mow
clover. I mow thick leafy alfalfa. I mow pungent sage
and wormwood, red-top, yarrow, bird's foot trefoil, blue
stem, quack grass, flaming brome. I mow up something
smelling like witch hazel, and something smelling
like honey. I mow up weevils, beetles, ladybugs.
Butterflies spin up from the header, from the scissoring
sections, pirouette in the updraft. I mow up
squirrels and mice and voles and shrews, green frogs
and grasshoppers, canary grass and devil trails.
I mow up cowlicks lapped by the wind's long tongue,
deer beds pressed flat in curving slumber.
The bitter smell of badger seeps up
from deep squirrel holes and catches on the reel.
(Yes, Virginia, there is a reel on my swather.)
Four rounds cut out the land, then back and forth,
north to south, south to north laying out windrows behind
like mare's tails combed out long and slightly wavy
all day long until it is done. And when light bends
the reflection on my slanted front window I mow up
black birds, cow birds, gray and white gulls, hawks
and buzzards soaring. I mow up ranch pickups,
stock trailers, compact cars, and big-deal eighteen-wheelers
passing on the road. (Thank goodness it's summer or
I might get a school bus or two.) I mow up
a vagabond strolling, long lines of willows lingering
by the creek, a wash hung out to dry, a barn's hot tin
roof, a whole mountain, thunderclouds building and
lots of blue sky to bale up into crackerjack bales
so when winter comes and the wires snap this day
will lay out on below-zero snow at the feet of our cows
and horses smelling of sunshine, saved up, returned,
woven in the warp of me.

2.

Through my swather's wide front window
I have a view beyond the thick grasses falling
before my sickle. Neighbors are in their fields
making hay all around me.
A baler there, and over there.
A balewagon stacking hay down there
beyond the silver poplars. Another swather
in the canyon's mouth and a combine
swollowing oats over there.
All at our own work, in our own way, yet
parallel, almost like a team.
I keep at it. Lunch is an apple and water.
After noon a few gulls fly in.


3.

Across the fence from where I cut grass
into lanky ropes of hay
cows watch as I pass,
spreading noise out behind.
Down the bench of a faultline
where water turns upward to the surface
is the sloped land where, one afternoon in the fall,
Mr. Jones died.

I stop the swather and cut the engine.
Haying means machines.
I accept the obliteration of natural sound
to hammering and clatter. But
as the engine settles into *not* working,
the noise drains slowly out of me.
The vibration lessens.
Silence reclaims me.


4.

Mr. Jones and his wife worked
digging out waterholes for their stock.
The eight-year drought would slip into history
once the rains began at the end of the month.

The land would live again.
But just now the cows couldn't wait
and who could know what was to come?

They rode his tractor across the fields.
She stood on the drawbar
in a pair of his old rubber boots,
one hand holding onto a #2 shovel,
the other — her husband's wide leather belt.
He sat the seat, slick as gut
and wobbling loose on a worn bolt hole.
They bounced and lurched
over dried out hummocks, grease woods,
and gaping cracks in the dry, dry ground,
working their way from one seep
to the next.

He stopped on the bench. They got off
and thrashed into the willow brush
to ditch water
through heavy black muck
where cows could get at it.
They worked most of the afternoon,
pounding the mud loose from the shovels on the sod.
Finished, they clambered out the way they came.
He sat down on the drawbar to catch his breath,
let the air get into him.
The sun was still high and hot.
She leaned on the shovel, weary, worried
what would become of them.
Everything was dying:
the trees, the fields, the land.
No rain. No rain.

He climbed onto the seat, pushed the starter
with the toe of his mud-caked boot.
The motor ground and caught. Said, Get on!
She did. He started off the slope. She grabbed
his shoulder, in a rough voice said to *back around!*

She wasn't *going off there!*
He said, Done it a hundred times, woman.
She said *you'll kill yourself.*
He shoved the throttle forward. She let go
and stepped off. One foot on solid ground,
the other coming off the drawbar
as if she pushed the tractor away.
The old man nosed it off the ridge.
The rough ground jerked the front tires,
the wheel from his hands, and pitched him
off the seat like a rag. The lugs
of the high tire took him down
and cleaned it's feet on his back.

The ambulance came across the field
turning lights — no siren.
She said, *I hope they don't start a fire
in this here dry grass.*
He said, *Ow,Ow,Ow*
when they rolled him,
slipped the clam shell underneath.
It took six of us to lift him.
The stretcher came up — thimble weed,
poverty grass in its teeth.
She said, *I told him he's crazy
to go off there.*
Told him he'd *tip that thing over
and kill hisself.*
Look there, if he hasn't gone
*and done it.*

5.
I drink warm water from the plastic jug in the toolbox.
A redtail hawk soars above me. The same one,
or a daughter, I have seen in this field for years
nesting in the locust tree at the old homestead
on the knoll above the granaries. Now she swings down
to claim a squirrel between the windrows.
Ravens pluck up field kill.

Gulls swallow dark furry mice whole, alive in one gulp.
Black birds work the windrows for insects.
Even the lovely redtail hawk is an opportunist.
She lifts off, squirrel swinging heavily.
At the nest in the locust two young hawks shriek
and hop, excited.

I lie down on uncut grass
until the service is over.

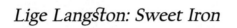

*Lige Langston: Sweet Iron*

# Duck Flat

My husband's grandmother left us a huge meat platter.
Large enough to embrace a twenty pound roast,
a leg of lamb from an old-cropper, a whole ham,
or two dozen quail nested in rice,
the sides of the platter scoop upward gracefully
to hold rich meat broth.

Her platter reminds me of Duck Flat, Nevada — of Lige.
Hand painted beneath the gold rim
before the final glaze was fired
is a lacy pattern
and mountains design the rim of the Flat
where Lige was born.

# The Claim Is Set

Lige tried to live an ordinary life
but he was born to the Flat
and it marks its own.
Not all, but some.

Pearl knew he needed more
than the Flat could give, more than
horses fat and fleshy, working
with his father hiring out in haying time,
shoveling gravel in the cart,
driving Chappo stop and go,
filling chuckholes in the road.

Burney turned his horses loose —
to trot, buck and run in play,
the mare nipping Chappo's neck,
until they drank and crossed the creek
and fed away.

Nine, when Lige went to Reno's school,
stared at plain wood walls,
dreamed of home on the Flat
waited for summer's smell.
He would help his father
hay their fields, Mike White's,
Uncle Dave's beside, hired out
at Mondo Camp, ran horses in
off Tuledad and Cottonwood,
and the Coppersmiths, if they strayed.

Lige lived an ordinary life
if you are born to the Flat.

## BELL RINGER

Doubtless
a bonnet and bell
identified the character of her caring
as the work of the Lord
but a widowed mother
(who made the work of laundry
— sheets and shirts and frocks —
into food for her six children)
ſtirred the soft shuffle of a bell
to remind passersby of their fortune.

She walked the boards of Reno's Bull Pen
to visit women living in cribs
waiting for men
to toss a brass token on the bed.

Their soft hands reached out to her ſturdy ones
for a flower from her bouquet
if the season was of flowers
and plucked friendship from her eyes
in any weather.

## To Make Amends

Pa's back moved in the rhythm of toil.
On the work bench the pocketknife
the boy borrowed from his father,
stepped on by the pan-footed Chappo,
bone handle splintered, spinning
on the rivet's brass pin.

Lige leaned 'round his Pa's shoulder
to see the vise grip a spike's antler,
first wracking of challenge, waxy light
and dark plug of growth rubbed lustrous
under velvet bark.

Steady, measured - shoulder, arm, saw
in a clean straight line cut the plate.
Chest pressed down hard
on the drill's wooden pommel
— bright curlicues winding up the bit stem.
Filed, dressed, seated on the pegs,
he burred the brads to hold.

The weight — right. The feel — right.
He opened the blade, closed the blade,
laid it on his son's palm.

Good as new, Pa. Better.

# GENTLEMAN

Pa came in from doin' morning chores.
The chicken house door was open
and all the hens were gone.
He looked until he found them
in the neighbor lady's chicken house.

"Did you get them back?" Mom asked.
"Well, yes," he said, "but I had to pay her for 'em."
"But they're *our* hens," she complained.
"I know," Pa said, "but she's a poor old lady."

# DEATH CAME RIDING

His fork smashed down against the saddle fork rising.
Forgetting turns. Forgetting doors. Forgetting faces.
Fifteen year old boy used to sagebrush and far country
walks beside his thin shadow on green walls

remembering horses, the jolt when they snatched their head,
the ache between his eyes, between his legs.
Nothing a horse did hurt like the thing waiting down the hall.

Four hundred miles from home. Wagon, horses tied outside
a city hospital filled with strangers.

His father's face floating between sheets and pillow,
already partly gone down dark halls. Stubble beard
dark in deep creases.

Safety razor, basin, soap.
Unscrew the head, unwrap the blade, lay it in,
twist it together. Pour water in the basin.
Lather the hard, square soap. Lay his hands on the face
he looked on with respect, loved
but had not touched since he was a baby.

Whiskers rough against his palms. Cool stiff skin.
Soap bubbles bleeding wet on the pillow. Razor scrapes
a clean, smooth swath down his father's tarnished face
who died before the shave was done.

# Coming Home on the Reno Train

Two washin' machines
waitin' on the back porch in the snow.
The kids said a man delivered 'em
for Mom to try.
Easywash and a Maytag.

It was a good deal.
Ten dollars a month to pay the thing off.
We decided on the Maytag.
I told Mom, we'll take in laundry.
I'll help, do anything Pa did.
I'll do anything.

Lige turned back to the Flat.
His long fingers combed horse hair
caught on the fence, began to braid
black over sorrel, grey over black,
sorrel over grey, over black again.

# Christmas On Ralston Hill

After Pa died
some folks from the Elks came to our house.
Of course when Mom opened the door
we all pushed around her
to see what was goin' on.
There were two women on our porch.
One handed a basket to Mom,
the other gave one to me.
It was heavy with food and toys
wrapped in fancy paper, tinsel and foil bells.
I can still remember how it smelled of ham,
spicy like cinnamon and cloves.
Well, you know kids, Oh boy!
but before we could touch a thing
Mom said in the softest voice,
"I'm afraid you've made a mistake.
There's a family right up the road
could really use these things."
She handed the basket back. I did the same.
Mom and us kids like a wreath around her.

# Trapline

One winter
fur was high.
Lige trapped bobcats
and coyotes,
lured them
to the jaws
of the iron trap
buried in the dirt.

He oiled the hinge,
filed the give-away spring
to a finite snap.
Wouldn't know what hit them
unless a foot hung,
then they had hours
to consider their error.
They had a life time.

He brushed his tracks out,
dowsed scent
just at the trap's tongue.
Wouldn't work
without the fragrance of heat,
bawdy piss
laced with blood.

He was too naive
to understand
there are all  kinds of traps,
scent, bait,
all kinds of hunters
as he stepped
deliberately
into the cunning circle.

# Pearly Everlasting

1. Newly-weds on the Flat

The cabin windows steamed with Francine cleaning.
From the barn Lige heard the door bang and bang
as she carried buckets of water from the pump
to scour herself into his life.

She strung lines from rafter to rafter,
washed all his clothes, starched his work shirts,
sewed neat patches over frayed holes.
She cut out recipes or invented them,
asked if he liked this or that?
He didn't know what they were
but he always said it sounded good
and gained ten pounds that winter
on light bread, puddings, cakes.

Evenings, she read the paper to him
while he cut long strings of rawhide
or mended gear
or they listened to the radio.
Sometimes they danced.

One night she made taffy.
They buttered up their hands and pulled it glassy.
He kissed the burned places on her arms
where the boiling sugar popped, tasting
the sugary butter slipping down her wrists.
Their first winter went by.


2. Day Work

Lige hired out to different ranchers by the day.
Come spring branding he stayed with the Marrs
better than two weeks. Lyle Cook

saw him on the road and sent him to Red Rock
and then it was somebody else
needing him. When he came home

her dress form stood in his place at the table.
She talked to it like he wasn't there.
He got mad, told her to cut it out.
She threw a stick of wood at him.

It was not the miles of sagebrush between her and everything.
It was not his hands that would be awkward now.
He brushed past her on the porch.
He'd take the first horse that came up from the meadow.
He hoped it wasn't that damned mare.


3.  Presser Foot

Her foot on the wide iron treadle.
The wheel turned. The needle pierced
the flat blue sky, traced the stem,
inched up the wild rose.

Her foot rocking on the black pedal
so wide she placed both feet together,
bare toes hooked in the scroll work,
knees brushing, pushing down,

the rocking pressure returned
a piston's throw, bobbin reeling
in the hood, making chains above
lock those below, sharp needle stitching
all the rose buds to the endless sky.


4.  Sunkist

At the windmill water gushed up
from the ground to fill the tank.
She cupped it from the pipe

to her face and throat, or unbuttoned
her dress
and lay out on the water
watching the blades
slice the sky into equal parts.

The dark bulk of the horses under the willows,
side by side, worried flies from each other
with a lazy swish of a tail. Those horses were Lige
and the Marrs boys waiting for the work
that would come for them.

She climbed the tower. A tin roof blinked hot
at the base of Mail Box Hill.
Too far away to see,
she knew Sunkist was there.


5. The Final Blow

She threw the windows open
so air could move the silence.

No screens. She searched the barn,
the shed, climbed into the rafters.
No screens.

She stretched a dish towel over the window.
Cotton muslin loomed tight to hold the silky slip of flour
would not yield to light, bellied in. She yanked it down.
All the world sucked into her deep vacuum.
Flies touched their feet to her loneliness.

Lige made a swatter from a scrap of boot top
laced to a willow stick, 3x4, small holes punched
in even rows. Air could pass through
but not the fly.
Limber leather. The handle end hit first,
alerted the fly to an instant of calm - a splendor-

before the final blow.

## 6. The Big Nasty

The gyp mine started up in the early '20's.
I worked loadin' buckets in the quarry all summer.
Oscar Daniels used a well rig to drill the holes,
packed 'em with black powder and they shoot the wall down.

Then I thought I wanted to do somethin' else
so I got a job runnin' the jack hammer.
Two of us. A little Eye-talian guy, Vince and me.

They called Gerlach the Big Nasty.
One guy said you'd see thing there
you'd never see any place else
and I guess he was probably right.

The Western Pacific was runnin' steady. Miners at Sulphur,
Leadville, silver at Hardin, gyp at Empire, sheepherders,
buckaroos all over the country and they all came to Gerlach
to let off steam.

## 7. Breathless

Francine lay
smooth as a pitcher of white enamel
pearlized by the sun,
turned to the wall
counting twigs cast in the whitewash.
He did not touch her
but listened
as if it was a love song.

# Desert Ranch Story

You might think, Oh, this is a horse story.
I've read this before. But it's not.
It's a story about a man
who rode many horses,
more horses than most remember
in all our dreams of horses,

used horses, their strength, speed,
their sense of how the world met end to end,
of lives shorter than most,
longer than some;

a man who cut the throat of a colt
with his pocket knife because couldn't leave it
falling behind, floundering, lost, dying;
a man gone dry of love for all things
but not dry of wanting love.

Three geldings, cut as colts, turned out
to grow, gathered in the Buffalo Hills.
One was the color of a bloody fox.
Unbroken, they swam in a circle of the corral
the rapids, the churn.
Man and horse in a silent dance, foot to hoof,
shoulder to body, mind flowed to mind,
thin as buffalo hide, one strand.
The blood bay stepped clear of the others,
from its own dream into the dream of the man.

He did not buck or waste time on fight.
He gave up such things for the man's smell,
touch, weight, pull of the bit on his tender mouth,
spank of the stirrup against his shoulder,
soft hat flapped over his eye, rope wisping
by his ears, and the gate opening to the Granites,
to the outside. At the top

the world laid out wider than can be imagined
if you have not seen the Black Rock Desert
and the Smoke Creek Desert touch and go on alone.

The year went by this way. Easy days
to begin, longer circles as summer moved on.
There were many horses in the man's string,
some tougher, some as honest, but he looked forward
to the blood bay.

At the end of day he unsaddled, led the bay to the pasture.
The bay did not gallop to the horses scattered, feeding
but walked to the sandy creek bank, folded his legs
to roll the day's work from his back, got to his feet,
shook, walked back to the man with his hand
on the gate, the rope looped easy along his leg.

## EAGLEVILLE DANCE

Whenever they had a dance in Eagleville
the place would be just packed till you
couldn't hardly wiggle and the first thing
you knew a brawl would bust out right
square in the middle of the floor! Nine
times out of ten Lige Langston would be
right in the middle just a sluggin' 'er out
with one of the Dees boys. Well, if the
band seen the fight start up, they'd stop
playin' the song they were on and strike
up "The Star Spangled Banner." Lige
would hear it and straighten up –
just like a man.

## Badger Camp

A man in camp
cooks different than a woman
— more grease poppin'
and a dust of flour
your boots track 'round,
a dipper hangin' by the water pail,
the dishpan sputterin, doin' a little dance
on the stove, the smell of the country
comin' in through the open door, coffee,
bacon carryin' down the meadow,
No extra dishes, no table scarves to mess up.
Jam in a jar and pancakes swimmin'
in the juice of stewed prunes and raisins
right on your plate.

## MAN TO MAN

Lige was always a gentleman,
even when there was just men around.
Never said anything off color. But one time
he gave me something to think about.
I came highballin' around the saddle shed
in a big rush and Lige was standin'
out there a ways with his back to me.
Like kids do I blurted out, "Whatcha doin', Lige?"
He looked over his shoulder as he buttoned up his pants.
"Shakin' hands with the unemployed," he says.

# For Forty Years

she ranted like a sow
when he threw his saddle in the pickup
latigo and cinches
lapping over the side

followed him down back streets
to see who he might visit
and how long he rested
his elbows on the gate

clawed onto the money
as if it had a meaning
and hardened to suppling strokes
that touched her in the night

was buried in the churchyard
in a grave of deep resentment
for her rivals who were horses
and freedom on the land

but when the hallway echoed
with the ring of profane silence
Lige sat in the evenings
of the long and bitter tears.

# Hooves of Horses

1.

Between Miller & Lux Spring and Horse Canyon
twisted in the brush, the hooves of a horse
still attached to the white, white of bones
by tendons dried, strands of caramel candy
pulled into tawny tapes against the marbled hoof,
tipped up, a bowl or cup holding a rim of rain
from the thunderstorm that graced us
and now sweeps east to Virgin Valley.

Hooves in even pairs, commisures
sidling the horny frog, heart-shaped,
frayed as gardening fingers, dry
as earth caked in the pretty curve of nail,
bars support the sole, wall thick
as a thumbnail is wide rounded
by lava rock, sand, smooth as if polished
with a chamois cloth.
A good hoof to travel on.

Two year old, or three, it's hard to say
but young and no more, dead, dismembered,
head just in view over there, spine
(here's the church, here's the steeple)
ribs wrenched open (see all the people?)


2.

How many hooves have I watched my father lift,
trim to track straight - stay sound, shoe?
I'd go along and turn the forge, air (my work drew)
turned iron red hot enough to bend, shape.
To those kids gathered 'round
(my father could draw a crowd from his cuff,

from behind my ear, from a wisp of cloud)
I held court, explained no, it doesn't hurt the horse
when the knife pares shavings, no,
rasp grates ridges level, no,
nails drive through the hoof wall
to hold the shoe in place. No,
I'd scoff with sudden upright posture,
them twice my size and I *so* wise.
I'd point out the *frog* knowing
they would not believe me saying *naaaw*
with eyes to my father who
- wedging horse shoe nails in his grip of mouth
like rays from sun - would shrug and nod.
*Ah*, I was bright for a small girl with palomino hair.
I'd lead the horse straight away, trot it back
so he could pleasure in a just, swinging stride.
How some old spoiled horse would drag on the me,
then he'd step up and spook it to a trot.
I'd go again, the horse improved in gait, set for work.
We'd go home, Dad and me, a team, a pair.
Him with money.  Me with pride.


3.

I caught up with John, him leading his horse,
the ground leading him from that swale
to that other drainage, from that hill
white with diatoms to that far one bare of brush.
In a place others regard as wasteland
he sees the shoreline of an ancient lake
alive with waterfowl, fringed by a Savannah
of palm, alder, fern, and meta sequoia,
(a museum tree in the Americas now,
but as a living tree, lost to humid Asia.)
He examines soil and bits of petrified wood,
patrols drainages for bones and teeth
of the beings that once flourished.
And he finds them.

We have boxes of them he works to identify
and understand - joints of camels,
giant ground sloth, jaws of rhino, deer, horses
and many still a mystery to him.
He has the artist's vision, sees things
others miss - same spot, same light,
same opportunity.

As a boy he struggled, caught between
this flicker of interest and ranch work.
Objects found were kept private,
in pockets, boxes under the bed.
(Children rebuffed grow tenderly secretive
and unstoppable.) He didn't know why
he felt at home, contented, inspired until,
in my discovery of the desert
he reached back to his own - open country.

He turns, a smile of *guess what I found,*
says *open your hand,* eyes say *are you ready for this?*
and in the basin of my palm — he pressed a thing —
half a walnut shell, I would describe it so.
*Can you guess?* he asked. Merychippus.
Late Miocene. Dawn Horse. Three-toed.
First grazer to harvest prairie grasslands.
Long limbs with fused ulna/radius,
tibia/fibula so it could gallop, turn
without twisting wrist and ankle.
Outdistanced predators like the bear-dog.
Point from which all horse lineage evolved,
extinct and living.

I knew hooves, held them in my palm
to clean, doctor, simply hold the curve,
so dense, so delicate, supporting
the weight of transition,
carrying the lifted stride of Merychippus
— Dawn Horse.
Hooves of horses. Flight of wings.
And this one.

# The Town Gossip

Francine was comin' up the sidewalk one day and Lige come along. He pulls that blue truck of his right over to the curb. The window was down an' he leans across an' says somethin' to Francine. I couldn't hear what it was a'course, I was clear up to the post office but she stands there lookin' in at him, stiff as a hoe handle. He was doin' all the talkin', I could see that. She's real thin, you know. Been doctorin' here lately. Haven't heard what for. But for all me, that drinkin' does take hold of a person after a while. Well, he reaches across the seat and the door swings open but she still just stands there for the longest time. Pretty soon she get's in the truck and Lige starts off up the street. Well, they didn't go fifty feet when here comes Etta right up behind 'em. She must'a followed him up from the ranch. You won't believe this, but she lays on the horn like she's callin' in for a fire and never lets off, no way! Everybody's gawkin' at 'em goin' up the street that way. I jumps into my rig and follows 'em too, so I seen the whole thing. Lige pulls right up to the hospital just as unconcerned as if he's out for a Sunday drive. He hops out and hurries around to Francine's side, opens the door, takes her hand and helps her into the hospital. Etta's out there just a poundin' on that horn. Well, some of the nurses come out to see what's goin' on but when they see its Etta they just flap their hands at her to shut it up and they go back inside. But Etta don't slack off one bit. Lige takes his own sweet time in there an' when he comes out he never even looks at Etta, just gets into his truck and drives off toward home. Etta's right after him, still layin' on the horn with both feet. Last I seen of 'em they was headed south. I wouldn't 'a' wanted to be in her shoes when he got her home, not for all the world. If they ain't a pair! That marriage was where the rattlesnake *met* the mule.

## C Section On The Barn Floor

You know. When you fit the chains
around the tips of hooves, slick, slimy tissue
torn where the hooves have presented themselves,
made their entrance. Hooves first,
like a diver except the dive carries this swimmer
from the depths of pre-life darkness, dull senses
through the passage - electric shock –
to break the surface of light.

You know. When you with your pounds of strength
pull against a thing as solid as the earth.
Slap the rope around your body below the waist
where the hips are solid and strong,
twist the rope around itself below your knees,
one, two, three, four and lift!
Can you lift the earth?
It's the complete resistance that collapses your will
within your brain and you know.

You could call the vet but he is miles away
and we understand how time can steal a life
as the rope unravels and the earth wins the pull.
And what would we learn for ourselves,
for the next time?

We gather the few necessary things
— shining stainless tools sacred
in our hands — so near they are to the saving of lives.
And thread. We'll need needles and strong thread.

The heifer is roped down. Legs tied like a tent tarp.
Somehow she disappears behind us and her stomach
becomes a bulge that is prepared quickly.
I won't tell you all, it's too long, but now,
the blade draws a parting line
from which small rivulets run blood

74

and it's on our hands.
The thick wall of tough tissue, striffing,
sinew that holds the weight of guts and calf
is a wave and through this opening I slide my hands.
Do you understand? I reach inside these living waters.

I won't explain the heat, and the pulse of organs
because I must hurry — the calf — I must find the sack,
the uterus and gently lift the weight of 80 pounds of calf
and many pounds of fluid up where I can cut the thing
that holds a life within a life.

One holds it. One opens it. The cut.
Take care not to lose a drop of the torpid sea
the calf is floating in. Eyes closed.  Waiting.

One tries hard to hold it. The slick heavy tough thing
that wants to leap like a fighting whale,
pull away from the hand reaching in to find a leg, hind leg.
The leg jerks back .— Don't touch me!
— and I can't help but smile.

Two legs up through this hole which opens on the sky.
A third person is needed here to take the calf
with block and tackle. Straight up! Carefully! Quickly!
Straight up until the head clears!
Cord taut, stretched, tearing like an air hose
on a diver's mask might snag on rocks and tear apart.

Third person tends the calf, clears the nostrils, mouth
of sludgey, rubbery fluid. The tapping within the ribs.
The head shakes and this huge slick fish
opens its eyes and it breathes.

But we are with the cow, now.
We two or three must hold the limp sack,
hold the uterus up and quickly sew it,
turning the edges in with the Lambert stitch,
pulling tight so it will mend,

so she can carry another calf in this stormy sea
that held her swimmer safe through time.

Then the stomach lining. Then the skin
and leave some space for draining.
She is untied and rolled upright. The calf,
her calf is pulled to her head to remind her
what this last 40 minutes was all about.
This calf too big to birth. 40 minutes
to save one life, to make one life.
And when she moos and licks the calf,
I say a prayer of thanksgiving.

We wash up. We wash her blood and fluids off,
unroll our sleeves, button the cuffs, unable
to take our eyes away from the calf struggling
wobbly wet to stand.
He bawls.
Her eyes brighten and she moos low and long.
She gets to her feet. He staggers down her side,
bumping her flank, ripening at her udder.

We go back to work. The work we were doing
before we felt that pull, as if
we were trying to pull the earth up
— between our feet.

# RESTING

I could not bear the dirt
clods broken apart one from the other
angry, wholly forlorn.
It was not the fertile ground a plow opens
before the drill files 'round, giving
seeds parting from the hull
capillaries tender reach — no.
A plot — the size of a man
laid out, sleeping, gaining strength
to rise up and work on.

Valley quail scratch the dirt for grit.
A meadow lark loops to the marker post,
gold larynx flared in intricate song.
Friends come and stand.

Rocks began to appear on the grave
shortly after the ground healed up
— hard flecked chunks from Granite Mountain,
Stone Corral's pink-cream churt,
the gauze of Empire's gypsum,
petrified wood from Badger, smooth
agate rolled down Tuledad wash.
What else could we bring?

Tangled in the rocks is a wild rose
that might be found in the desert anywhere
— sweet pink flowers, thorns,
scarlet hips. Seeds.

*Ride the Silence*

# Quiet Land

1.

We who are content living scattered
We who have grown used to the tension of the wind
We who lift our corner of the sail
        have the plain faces of time.


2.

Some seeds need the crack of freezing darkness
Others seek the warmth of wintered over leaves
Some flowers trust the bee to carry pollen
        others risk the wind.


3.

Within the shelter of golden grasses
Within the quiet of land that lives alone
There are the wings of locust
        and the call of the mourning dove.


4.

There is remembrance.
There is the journey.
There is the air that breathes between.

## SWANS

I let the swans float gently
on the blue gray sheen of the lake
though my secret wish is to be among them
grooming my own slim feathers.

The water is beneath.
Their black webbed strokes move them.
The sky is above.
Strong wings keep them moving there.

And when it is time
they rise above the lip of the lake.
High up the land and trees and water fade.
The earth is a tan and blue haze.

They see nothing but the simple air
and draw forward.
Some water clings to them
and some sky.

## GOLD MUSTARD

Oh! we were in a hurry that day
        the list was long
I rushed beside you in silence

Chores before dawn
        horses saddled
        standing tied in the old barn, ready
Trucks squatted, swaying with the weight of cattle
        nose to tail at the chute
        cows, calves exploded from the doors
        bawling
First the branding
        every empty loop caught a look of hurry in it
        every move cut in half     half smiles

        Hurry, open the gate
        drive them to the pasture
        ride the fence

until we came to the fawn
curled on the ditch bank
under a mustard bloomed gold

The doe was hidden in the willow thicket
        her caged eyes betrayed the small and perfect fawn
We held our breath as if the mere taking in of air
        might hollow out the moment
In full sun there was the mark of speckled shade across its back
        licked in swirls
        the string of raw cord
        only a trace of dampness on the dirt

        to lie perfectly still
        from the most passive womb
        not taught   no thought
        known as four legs are known

as hardening hooves are known
as the murmur of muzzle
and tongue removing any trace of birth are known
it remained still

# THE FIELD OF THE OWLS

Today we gathered the heifers from the hot springs field.
Only a few hundred acres, but a maze of hot bogs
the cows have charted.

Owls flew up from the thatch soundlessly, like moths
circled where a heifer stood off.   Her calf, half buried with snow
was dead.

Reluctantly she left it
and joined the long strings of cows on their secret trails across
the marsh.
She turned and started back several times.

At home I spread a bale of hay in the shelter of the barn
for three young cows, their calves and her.
The cows waited while I jostled calves — limber as noodles —
from the trailer.

I checked them before going to the house.
Three cows stood with their heads in the hay.
Three calves nursed.   She stood separate
gazing far — where the owls feed.

# DROUGHT

In the midnight she woke.
It was not the window rattling against dry putty
or wind pulling and sucking the back door
or the thump of the stove cooling.

Deeper.
It was the ache of dying trees and land.
It was cattle waiting by dry ponds.
It was his stillness beside her in the dark.

It was the sound of no rain.

# Playing At Doctor

Poor old broken legged ewe,
the flop of it wrings my stomach,
the grate climbs my spine like a stair.
Three strong legs are tied
so I can mend the one that snapped
when the shearer yanked you under the curtain.
Your eyes are closed.  Your breath
blows the dirt smooth as I wind the gauze
up and down, up and down the cedar splints.
Without a scan I find alignment with my fingers
and hope your muscles will pull the bones tight.
I roll you to your feet and fight you to a stall
where you stand on three and blame me for your pain.
Your plaster stiffens my hands to hooves.

# On The Raft Of This Day

Sometimes I come up against it
flattened like a moth outside a window
wanting in where the light is.
My palms press the questions
smutty with sweat and I look hard
into slurred movement, shadows
slipping through each other
as my fingers slip through sound.

I try to get back away from the glare
so I can see what the tricks are
so I'll know when to duck or step aside.
It works for the small things
choosing two shoes that match
or sweeping crumbs into a pan
but the big picture is out of focus.

Instead of a view
I am overtaken by the blend of colors
and I content myself knowing the land lays out
in a kind of union
whether I ask or not.
The direct flight of migrating geese combs through me
and I feel the brush of each gray feather.
They are paired up as they move north
trusting Spring.

# In The Evening Autumn

As I rode out to check cows calving
the light came across the meadow low
soft
and in it
I could see a shimmering blanket of cobwebs
moving in the breeze
like the surface of water.

The whole of the meadow
under billowing silk.

While I go about my singular life
an army
of small spiders
has set about to hold this entire world together
in a veil of fine silver strands.

# The Cure

I prescribe you this —
go to the desert
high or low,
cold or hammers of Hell

shed the clothes of care
strip down to the bones
step out brave
let the desert see you're unarmed
and only ask for time

to hear the song of sage
turn green leaves silver

laugh out loud
or sing
those sounds are welcome here

rest
sleep until you numb the earth
we all must have our time
and yours is now

# First-calf Heifer

Lying flat   resting
between heaves of labor's force
glaring over her shoulder at me
suspicious of me crouching in the grass.

Magpie on the ribs of a winterkilled cow
sings the song he's practiced
then changes to a whir, chuckle
burble like a faucet cracked.

We both wait while the sun
strikes heavy on my bare arms
and turns his lean black coat to dark teal silk
against a ruff white as bone.

Toes push out.  Toes suck back.
Trefoil grows an inch.  Water has time
to run uphill.  I am guilty with the snap
of her teeth grinding and the violence of her labor.

The magpie wants the blood rich placenta.
I want a breathing calf.
My knife cuts long curls of pale willow flesh.
The magpie sharpens his black beak on the hump of skull.

# Give Us Rain!

Don't we wait for rain in this dry country
licking down sweet wild kisses,
pretending it's not our heart's desire?

If rain was a person
we'd have given it up long ago as shiftless,
a worthless uncle, a tawdry aunt
— we've had both —
and still, when they come walking up the road
suitcase swinging,
hat cocked to shade one eye,
we beam a smile — the mirror of their own,
hear stories of their roaming,
sticking our tired old feet deeper into the sucking earth
that owns us,
our callused hands deeper in our pockets
where nothing jingles.
They whisk off too soon,
just a scent of store perfume on the pillow
pressed to my face.

I can't help but notice the persuasion of the clouds,
calves playing extra frisky, and that smell
directly after —
hope is all I know.

Light, it pit-a-pats on the barn roof like kittens playing.
Then it comes swifting down
holy water blessing the meadows alive, us alive.

Pretty soon it's pounding and my chest is tight.
Colts dance to the hammering on the tin,
pulling back against their halter ropes with white rimmed eyes.
Cattle buck and run to the trees, us to the porch.

Oh! we've missed you, rain!    Give us more!

Fill the tanks!
Lap the banks!
Wake the seeds!
Even weeds!
Drown the fish!

More hay!    Meadows jumping!
Turn those skinny old cows into butterballs!

Don't you know how happy we are to see you, beautiful old
rain?
God!    We are happy!

# Dat So La Lee

*Washoe master basket maker*

Stepping through a willow patch
long stems comb the sky
      slender brown fingers touch
      slender red stems.

The air in a simple phrase
holds her upon the earth
where her people gather.

She splits the reed between her teeth
to release its will
and each strand follows her hands in arcs
      antelope before the bow
      flared wings of the sage grouse dance
      butterflies that wake to wings
      clouds that turn to oyster shell
      pinon giving harvest.

She knows the calling of the reed to bend.
She knows the power that rides her.

# How Tom Became A Cowboy

In memory of Tom McCoy

He looked at me
decided to tell the truth
not that old story he pretended was true.

My folks died when I was four.
I was sent to live with an uncle and aunt in Canada.
I was put on a train in Red Bluff.
A black woman was paid to watch me.
I was scared when she set me on the toilet over the tracks —
I could see down through the hole.
I refused to use the toilet.
I messed my pants.
She slapped me.
A man came into the toilet and saw her.
He pushed her away and washed me up.
He took care of me all the way to Canada.

My uncle and aunt put me in a back shed.
A black dog slept in the shed with me.
They told me the dog was mean and not to touch him.
I was afraid to get off the bed.
I waited until he was asleep to use the water closet.
Their girl brought my food.
After many days I hugged the dog.
He didn't bite me.

When I was ten I took a horse and saddle as my earning.
I rode away.
I found work as a cowboy.

He stirred his coffee and drank it cold.

# Inside Straight

He loved her long horse face and eyes
cocked bright and waxen.
Her mouth fell open to bray out joy
and her long legs wrapped him warm
like no quilt could.

He was a silent horseman.
He held to his woman with the same kindness
in his touch, patient with her small gifts
      of a turning head
        an ease about the shoulders.
It was enough for him.

But it was not enough for her.
She had no feel in her hands, no thread
to head or heart.  The lash
was never laid across *her* long hip.
Spurs never tasted blood on *her* belly.

The man she wanted had hair sprouted from his ears
but his fences ran farther than she had ever ridden
and the big corrals could not hold his cattle.

She burned his car through the tight-lipped town
to shop the big stores on the river,
dropping tips as if waiters deserved them.
She worked, oh, she worked
and filled his old home with a noise
that came close to happiness
for a while
and he loved her
for a while.

But in time she slipped beneath the arbor
to meet the hired man.
Two thieves drove the desert

and let long shadows of betrayal
sweep a blur of darkness.

When widow's weeds flowered in her garden
she took the hired man to the big house
and pushed her clothes aside to give his room.

They cut a short swath but wide,
spinning off on the good-time highway,
whittling the ranch toothpick thin.
And a young dog will roam when the breeze blows right.

She took to her bed with the ghosts of her men
who drew back when she laughed
and brushed out her long graying hair.

# Uncle Ben On The Bench

Every afternoon, they say
trembling with disease, cane
tapping, whispering against his rough jeans
a code, a message — I can't tell.

A plain open hillside watches him
above the town where houses crouch
and people feared him young.

Every afternoon, they say
running horses, beaded gauntlet gloves, and
anyone's woman he could beguile — his dark eyes
tossed the heat of lightning.

Bloody fists behind the dance hall.
Boots on the kitchen table dared
husbands to ask.

Someone should have killed him, they say.
Instead, he has a bench facing the bare hillside
where horses ran, his whip lashing the wild sky
his cane, whispering.

# A Rancher

In memory of Lawrence Parman

We lost the ranch
in the 30's.
We were flat broke.

I ran a trap line
for cash.
Sold my hides in Gerlach.
The man gave me a check.
I didn't know if the check was good
but I had to take the chance.

Well, there was no place to cash a check in Gerlach.
No money a'tal
so I jumped the train for Reno.

I went straight to the bank.

The check was good all right.
I did a little shopping
and bought a ticket on the afternoon train.

Rode home like a gentleman.

# Ride The Silence

This land asks for quiet passion.
The surface still, beneath
a thunderous shake
of underground rivers grinding
through bed rock of the earth's own form.
No one knows the torment knotted,
gnarled beneath their daily feet.

Life on this land where we tend stock
against relentless heat and tearing storms
must be steady.
We ride the crust of earth with its hot arteries
flowing molten stone and we are calm
we are silent and watch the land as a placid sea, biding
agonies that will undo blouses and trousers of the depths.
Passion chained back
when ice storms blow snow down throats of cows —
they drown on white and frozen land.
Or sickness cuts the tally,
or men of power bleed the poor ones pale.

The torture turns passion to petty heights,
pulls the juice,
the raging juice that lies below —
lets it loose when night comes
and no one hears the back door close.

# The Man Shoeing a Horse and His Little Girl

He whirled those blue eyes on me
flat blue eyes
bottomless eyes
where the pupil had shrunk up
so he was only seeing through that
pinhole
screwing me down like a microscope
seeing into me past awkward
structural uprights, joist and 2x4,
past electrical wires running, past gray
puttied pipes, past insulation, wall board,
paint, plaster, and chimney into
the real center – the blueprint where angles could be altered
to add or subtract things,
and I felt myself shrinking, all jellied with no legs to run

but those eyes
in that face flushed red by his frustration and the hoof ripped
through his knees
seemed to wash calm
the pupil coiled out and was the dark seeing center
with the thin blue wall
no more x-ray vision

and those blue eyes
ran over me like warm honey
smeared me
the rasping palm
soft
smoothed me out so I wasn't sorry anymore I asked the
question
and he
in that voice
I could pull on and wear
spoke

# In the Yellow Hills

Horned toad hiding
beneath a swag of dusty sage.
Your eyes of mirror
say you're not there at all.
Armor plated softy,
the prickles on your skin
will bend against the softest sigh of wind.

A rock that waddles.
A skipping stone with legs.
You would fit perfectly in my hand
and feel my heat against your cold leather.
But that would change you
— it would change me.
You would speak of warmth
to a silent, frosty night

and I would not be there
to offer my cupped palm.
I can't say where I might be
moving my own armored shell
across the sand.

# FATE'S GIRL

In memory of Sid Harris


Somewhere between the cuff and the hem
of life's dark coat
there lived a man.
Not a man who — as example — your father
comes to mind but a father all true of a girl
slight and plain to see.
The flat brow of her pale face furrowed
for lack of joy and old eyes with chilling calm
expected no better than they'd seen.

They traveled the low road over the '49 Trail,
the man Fate — and his girl.

Now Fate was a man of low ambition
with an eye quick for opportunity,
his habits — tasteless, his wits sharp
and guided by a devil plan.
He avoided the symmetry of convention
and if ever right and wrong wrestled an issue
in his head the bout was short and right
laid low, blind-sided.

On the trail Fate used some greasy ploy
to wrench a weighty pouch from a fellow traveler.
Fate was not a particular man
and whether the traveler laid the night
in drunken dreams and woke a plucked bird
or didn't wake at all
only Fate and his little daughter knew.

The girl — and we must call her that
for he gave her nothing, not even a name,
she followed him
seeking life's need unnoticed, uncared for
a thin, weak shadow he cast in the dark of night.

She followed him
not by design but habit led her
by the balance of abandonment
and hanging like a burr
to the hide of a marauding dog
not knowing the path or the choice.
She followed him.
Not knowing right — wrong came right for her.

They stopped in an empty shack, a shallow canyon,
one room, a trellis of moldy blanket roped off
private quarters and with the stolen bank roll
Fate stocked the shelves with whiskey
— he did not buy the girl a coat or shoes.
Fate knocked together a bar
— he would not make the girl a bed.
In town, he took chairs from behind the church
and a table from the school.

As her father
he took command of her time and service.
She swept up, hauled wood and made meals.
And when buckaroos tied tired horses outside,
Fate's Bar was open for business.

They stopped by.
Curiosity and having news to tell forced them to.
They reported a sorry place
but others went to see for themselves.

Fate set out a bottle
measured each man with his black eyes,
slid shaved cards from his pocket,
and planned how to take their money.
When he saw their mood turn sour
and feared of losing their gold to places in town
he pushed *her* toward them.

She watched gold's glint pass from palm to palm
and found that *she* changed hands.

No horse could outrun this tale of madness.
No shame ever born could stand beside.
The wooden shack might well be made of daggers
sharpened points thrust outward
or pox, or witch's sign
for the only ones to turn their horse to Fate's Bar
were uncut strangers on the '49.

Among them was a horseman
slightly built and young of heart.
Of life his tastes were not full taught,
for chance was slim. He was fond of God
and God of him as his smile was well at hand.
Troubles few beset this lad and troubles few he gave.

On an early morning in the cool of Fall's last dance
he came upon Fate's girl on the spine of a barren hill.
Caped by blowing hair, leaving barefoot tracks
in earth soft by dew she went fast
as if to outrun her own skin.

Weeks went by.
He left his cattle grazing free to find her in the hills
bringing a kitten from the woman at the general store
— yellow with white mitts — meant as kindness.
But she shied like a colt
so he tucked it beneath his heart and rode away.

On another day she took it from his hands
scarcely touched him as her fingers curled in yellow fur.
Muted by circumstance
her eyes gave back the gift of blue and tears.
His own eyes held her strong, to reappear in dreams.

On a certain icy day with a gun swung from leather
the bold boy pressed by anger rode direct to Fate's Bar.

There he was witness to the fate of Fate
and it rides him heavy still.

Horses waited around the shack. Door thrown wide,
rowdy men hoisting bottles, shooting guns,
shouting fit to bust, they grabbed him by the collar,
dragged him to the bar — Drink up, old son,
don't lift your purse, the drinks are on the house !

The boy jerked free, his purpose not for fun
'til they showed him Fate eyes as cold in death
as in life, belly up across the poker table
six round burns gathered where his heart would be.
The kitten sprawled on the bloodied floor
yellow head bent back wrong.

Nobody knew who did it. Nobody
seemed to care. They raged the party on and on
'til they wrung the bottles dry,
broke the last for Fate,
flared a match across a thumbnail
and watched the flame take life.

Cold wind brought snow along the '49
wiped tracks from sight
sputtered as it hit the embers.

When he tired of staring into the fire
he took himself away
rode through a curtain of snow to a silence
where he hoped to forget
what he had seen and what he knew.

Did she consider life and death
and that hairline of purpose separating the two,

stand near enough to smell Fate's biled contempt
hear his heart give one last tick
see the awful surprise in his eyes

when winged truth
of what he was and what he was to be
settled on him like death birds at dark

we will not know
for she is gone.

## On The Waiting Land

There is a desert
it is mine
and it is yours
> *badger*

Quiet lives there
rent free
> *raven*

Sun comes nearly every day
and if it doesn't
> *rock chuck*

the desert waits
and thinks of the sun
> *red tailed hawk*

Things live in the desert
> *blue bird*

— with quick steps and silent drift.
> *golden eagle*

Then, light slips across each leaf of sage,
> *kangaroo rat*

each gray stem
> *horned toad*

down the shredded bark
> *rattlesnake*

and sips the snow.
> *ermine*

Clouds roam
beyond borders of humor
        *chipmunk*

and gratitude
and grace
        *antelope*
and crisp shadows
        *peregrine falcon*

where aspen willingly shimmer
        *mule deer*

if wind decides to follow.
        *snow shoe rabbit*


There is music
in the pale of dawn
        *sage grouse*

or the plowing snows
        *kit fox*

the calm of noon
        *lark*

or in the echoing stillness
of evening
        *coyote*

as stars rub
and spark
against the pace of night.
        *burrowing owl*

        porcupine

        beaver

packrat

blacktailed rabbit

magpie

prairie falcon

## Desert Crossing

Willows follow the river's twist up the valley.
Horse tails blown on south winds
brush the sky toward the finish line.

The desert turns its endless face
to cars whizzing past.
It doesn't care.

This was once a great, wide plain.
Herds flowed across
on tidal cuts of the great land-sea.

But the earth has the last word.
A foot kicked up under the big blanket
knocking elephants and rhinos to Africa,
shook llamas south of the equator
and took the bridge.

We came along, put up signs,
hung out the wash,
jacked the old truck up on blocks,
and we think we're sleeping on bedrock.

## Did You Forget

The sky was startling clear.
Only a few stars
bright with heat cooled long before we held hands here,
before there was such a thing as love.

How can it be seen
long after the passion incinerates,
disperses into vapor?
The physics of it doesn't matter.
There will be this moment burning brilliant
in some other night.

# GREAT BASIN

In this space — this open-ness
where light feels its way along the hills
close
there is room for knowing

The landscape repeated
the silence living  —  being  — just the same
as the place where the light turns

At any moment — here
the most uncivilized among us
could unmire their bones
from the earth
from the sky
and begin again.

Own the land.
Walk the boundary.
Stack stones.
Stake it out.
Mine — the footprints speak.
Mine.

And with the deepest blood
not from the fingertip
where it turns nearly rusted through
not from the wrist
where the vein is blue as iced water
ropey, snarled around the Devil's ankle
not from the inside bend of elbow
that rolls soft against your woman's waist
not from the neck
stem to where this desire was brewed

but from the heart
the most fragile skin a knife can pierce
with just the outmost tip
and once the skin is rent
the pump will thrust as if its pumping water against a fire
its leak unchecked
unseen.

From this score
is where you dip the quill
and sign
not    *man of earth*
but name yourself
for claim is twin to that blood now dried to tint
and of no further use

and still the pump labors on
and fills your tracks

until you run dry and drop like leaves
and there will be the feel of other feet
upon your fields.

# CRANE

A thing of flight
standing in the reeds
touches my heart.

The lame leg
hangs.
I know him each year.

*Where the Wind Lives*

# Under The Hunter Moon

I slip the rifle sling over my shoulder
      and step into the silence of dawn
Geese move through the darkened sky
      toward the pond
      Wings cut the quiet
      with an oddly mechanical sound
      and then their voices set me right

I open the gate
The sheep rise from their beds
      as if I commanded it so
      Lambs rush to thump flanks for milk
      kept warm through the autumn night

I fall in with their march up the meadow
      to find clover that grew while they slept
Stalks of blue chicory and tiny golden trefoil
      fold inside pink lips, and chewing,
      they walk on

At the fence line I know the place
      where soft pads left prints in the dust
      by a hole in the woven wire
      and I am a warrior hunched in rose briars
      their scent pale, and their thorns pick at my wool coat

Stern in my resolve
      I wait while the sun creeps to the edge of the day
Slain lambs, guts ripped open
Magpies and blow flies
Blatting ewes with swollen bags searching the flock

A lamb a day for two weeks
      I grip the rifle tighter

A shadow comes toward me through the moonlight
     grey and tan, she arches in a mouse pounce
     and works her way toward the barrel of my rifle,
     toward the bullet I will hurl
     at her heart


I watch her snatch mice out of the grass
     flip them up like popcorn,
     down the hatch.  She is a comic
     this coyote, playing, laughing
     making her way steadily toward me
     my finger soft on the cold steel trigger

Coyote stops
     looks directly at me
Her eyes hold me accountable

The following poem, "Homesteaders, Poor and Dry," proved to me the power of stories.

As a part of the Nevada State Art Council's Tumblewords project I was invited to take poetry to the French Ford Middle School in Winnemucca, Nevada. My audience was to be fifth and sixth graders. Carolyn Dufurrena, the homeroom teacher, met me in the hall. She asked, "Will you read them the poem about the well."

I was surprised. Although it was a true story, I thought it a dark poem, not something I would present to innocent children. "Are you sure?"

"Yeah." she said. "You have no idea how bleak some of their lives are. I hear some pretty shocking stuff from them. Read it."

There was one small boy in Carolyn's class that reminded me of a boy in my fifth grade class: small, tough, and separate, somehow. William moved through knots of his classmates as if they were of another animal class or phylum, or as if he were. The other children politely took their seats. William climbed up on a desk beside me and sat cross-legged on the tabletop, elbows on his knees, chin resting in his palms. The teacher did not ask him down, to sit properly in the chair. He stared into my face with an air of suspicious expectation, as if he hoped I might tell him something useful.

I worried that the poem might register as abusive, brutal, at the very least. Carolyn sat in the back of the room. Her face was calm. I had to believe she knew what she what she was doing.

The classroom was perfectly quiet as I read the story a friend had told me of an incident in her grandmother's life when she was just a girl. It is a moving story of empowerment, of conquering fears. Afterward, some of the children gathered around me. Some asked questions. Some were contented to just hold my hands.

Without a word, William got down from the desk, boosted his backpack onto his shoulders and went out the door.

On the drive back to my motel Carolyn told me that she's sure that William is abused at home. He comes to school with bruises on his face and thin arms. He has had broken bones. Some days he is so distracted he won't speak at all. Once, word reached her that both William's parents were gone and he was taking care of the younger kids of the family. She stopped by to check on him. When she saw there was no food in the house, she went back with a bag of groceries. She never asked for a note from his mom.

In an essay assignment William wrote that he lived in an abandoned mine in the hills above town. She dismissed the story as a boy's imagination taking flight, though she knew the foothills area is a dangerous maze of abandoned mines. She read the story again of him slipping under boards at the mouth of a mine, scurrying along the tunnels like a mole to the pocket where he kept a stash of matches, a candle, food and blankets, where he sleeps safe within the earth. Now, she thinks it might be true.

# Homesteaders, Poor and Dry

The world was bone dry.
I don't know why God would do such a thing.
The field was bare as the floor
And the springs nothin' — nothin'.

Papa's cattle bawled night and day
    'til I thought I'd go crazy with it.
    Turn them out, I cried.
    Kill them, Papa, I begged.
    And he did.
    And he killed himself, too
    in a way
    'cause he loved them crazy ol' cows.
I had to help him.
    There wasn't anybody else.
    Momma had the baby.

He handed me the big knife
    and I followed him.
First he took the red one,
    the one he didn't like the most.
    Old Mule, he called her 'cause she kicked him every day.
He coaxed her into the barn.
She went hoping for some hay.
The barn still smelled like hay,
    so she went.
He tied her up
    and took the knife from me
    held it 'round behind his back.
    He thought she'd know what he was up to,
    and run.
He slipped his arm around her neck
    and the knife came up
    sharp and glinting
    like a present.

His hands were shaking.
He had killed cows and pigs and chickens
       millions of 'em
       but his hands were shaking now.

This dry had him half crazy too.
Just when I thought he wouldn't do it
       he screamed
       and I screamed
       and old Mule screamed.

       She pulled back
       and her wild eyes looked right at me.
       Blood thumped out of her and she fell
       shaking the ground under me
       as if I was going, too.

Papa was on his knees crying,
       I'm sorry, old Mule, I'm sorry,
       and I ran away.
I threw the gate open
       and chased the other cows away.
       I didn't know where they'd go,
       but somebody else could kill 'em.
       Not my Papa.

The next week the well went dry.
Papa would drop the bucket down
       and it would come up empty.
He turned the bucket over and the bottom was wet.
He said I'd have to go down in the well
       and fill the bucket
       with a cup.
       I'd have to
       'cause we could never pull him up.
       He was the strongest
       and the well was small
       and I was the smallest.
       No Papa. I can't.

Yes, you can, girl.  You can do it for the Baby.
He tied a stick in the rope
      for me to stand on
      and boosted me over the side.
      I could only see a few feet down
      then there was a black hole
      and I was looking into the belly of a monster.
      A monster that would take me in one swallow
      and I didn't even get to have my own baby and home yet.

His face brushed mine
and I whispered, No Papa.
      No.
      But the rope was sliding down over the edge
      and I was going down too.
I clung on to that rope
      nothing could get me loose.
There were things down there.
      Scarey things that would touch me.
      Papa's face in the circle of sky went farther away
      until I couldn't see him
      only a black circle in a blue circle
      getting smaller.
The well was so narrow
      the walls brushed me.

      It was dark
      and places big rocks stuck out and scraped me.
      I cried let me up
      let me up
      but I was still going down,
      leaving the world
      leaving Mama crying my name
      and my Papa moaning, it's for the baby, girl.

I was lowered down in that well every day
      'til the drought broke.
      Every day.

I closed my eyes and sang myself songs
dipped the water raising down there in the pitch dark
all by the feel.
But there was no time I'll remember like that first time.

After, when the water came back up in the well
I went and looked down into the water
and imagined myself on the bottom
and sometimes I wanted to go back down
to the quiet of the dark.

In all my life
nothing can make me scared.
I went down into the earth
and drew back up.

Nothing can ever scare me again.
No man.
No beast.
No God.
I saw His face that day
and He promised me
no fear.

The second story of "Homesteaders, Poor and Dry" is this:

*After reading the poem at the 1995 Cowboy Poetry Gathering in Elko, Nevada, an attractive older woman approached me in the hallway of the Convention Center. She had the look I'm used to seeing in ranch women, unpampered self-assured, capable, direct.*

*These meetings after readings are often an ego boost to writers. We dearly love to be told how our wonderful poetry is meaningful, a rare delight, and are ready with a humble reply or a pen for an autograph.*

*This woman did not bother with compliments. Without so much as an introduction, she asked, "Was that you in that well?"*

*"No," I replied. "A friend's grandmother."*

*Her eyes filled and in a voice husky with emotion she said, "Well, it was me."*

*Like William, she turned and was gone. But in those brief moments I beheld an opening of the human heart.*

# I Fix the Fence – the Fence Fixes Me

The fence I patched ran away
rolled a week ahead.
Ahead.
My horse along for company, we sang
my horse and me
Yippie-ti-yi-yo

so my horse and I would know
this work — this fence assigned to me was just a lark
for I could see
there were no other ones this free,
just him and me
and air
that danced with Spring
going in
and loaded down with dreary Winter
freed me with each sigh
Good-bye.

Fence work is pointed sharp,
makes me look tight at wire frayed,
staples sprung, wood posts splayed.
As morning raced on mended wire
I began to tire
of all this freedom, and my horse's songs ran dry.
Spring's snap became a plod,
the sun burned hot,
the water gone. I thought of home and company
then felt the wire
take a bite of me
and I looked smaller still to see
how deep a barb can tear, when
bluebirds —
bluebirds, blue as sky, bluer
than a baby's eye, blue as

love's reply — flit, (not fly)
from sage to sage
on flicker wings, and sing
*Cheer. Cheer lee churn*
each one in turn.

Well —
what is there for a buckaroo
to do
but blush a bit
at nature's wit
and blow a kiss
to birds so blue
they leave the sky behind.

## The Blue Filly

She is just three.
Weaned again.

First time from her mother
        small blue head
        in the flank of a still heart.

Second time from a spotted burro
        who let her stand near
        as they swept flies in their head-tail sleep.

Last from the mare band
        that taught her with stinging nips
        to stand back and wait.

She sees him coming.
        Hay poking out in mid-chew
        does she wonder, "what now?"

He speaks her name
in sound and breath
she will come to know as her own.

A halter slips over her nose.
        She follows him into the barn
        shivering.

Hobbles hold her
        while the brush sweeps
        firm and soft over her skin

and when his hand slides down her neck
        I feel it on mine.

We both relax
and prepare ourselves for the saddling.

# Dear Child

We gathered the desert in June
to brand calves born since turn-out
as moved them up the mountain with the feed.

June is hot.
Days are long.

Ride a wide circle
         gather toward a gate
         brand the afternoon away
         trot to camp, supper, bed.

I worried about Katie,
         our tiny girl of seven.
But she pushed Smokey near a rock,
shinnied up his old leg
and rode out among the buckaroos.

Katie and I rode across Butcher Flat
         swung toward Sarvis
         pushing cattle up Shoestring.
I sent her to the ridges
         into sudden draws
         for a break from pecking along behind
         small calves keeping up
         little hocks brushing, tails swinging
         on the trail the branding fire.

Early afternoon — choking dust,
         heat waves dancing, smoke drifting,
         over the bawling herd —
         the branding started
Katie croaked, "I'm thirsty."
         But that was in my
         words-of-wisdom period, I said,

"There's no use complaining, dear child.
We're all thirsty
and hungry, and tired.
When the work is done
          we can rest.
You don't hear anyone else say,
          'I'm thirsty.'
Saying it makes us all twice as thirsty.
Hold on. We'll be done soon."
We finished the day.
Trotting back to camp
Katie, strong in the middle
learning how buckaroos
only tease the kids they like.

She had a water fight in the spring
ate two helpings and dessert
          fell asleep sitting up at the table.

I tucked her in the bedroll,
          kissed her sunburned cheeks and said,
          "You were perfect today."
          In her own wisdom, said,
          "No, Mom. Not perfect,
          ...almost perfect."

Some day, to her small boy
          she'll say, "There's no use complaining,
                    dear child."

## Love Letters

Wow!
was written in the dust
on the bedside table.

The dawn and I blushed together
as your spurs
chinged
around the kitchen
as you started the fire.

I stretched full length
on the cool smoothness
of the sheets,

a kept woman
a moment longer.

Within an hour's time
we'll be ahorseback
in a long trot
to some distant blue mountain
hunting cows.

I'll carry your message
close
knowing there will come a day
I would give a year of my life
for that ...
Wow!

In 1994 I was invited to read at the Indian Village Restaurant in Lakeview, Oregon. I intended to include The Widow Olson in the reading because I thought it would be of historical interest to the people of that region. The poem describes a trail drive of 5000 head of cattle that took place in the southeastern quarter of Oregon, in the dead of winter, early in the 1920s, from the MC Ranch in Warner Valley, across Hart Mountain to Frenchglen at the base of the Steens Mountains.

During a hard winter following a dry summer the MC ran short of feed. There was an abundance of feed at Frenchglen. After the murder of Peter French in 1897, the ranch had changed hands several times. The new owners had not yet stocked the ranch and were willing to sell off the old feed. The MC crew only had to drive the cattle there.

Jimmy Washoe, the MC horse wrangler, was just a kid in the 20s. In 1991 he retraced the drive – this time with John and me in our pick-up. He told us how Pete French drove the Indians from the valley with a bullwhip and, with a sly smile, he told us that they came back and burned down a barn. He took us to see the famous Round Barn French had built so his hired men could work horses through the winter. A massive juniper tree is the center pole of a structure shaped like a circus tent. French built three such barns. Only one remains. And only Jimmie remains of the MC buckaroos who drove horses and cattle across Hart Mountain to the P Ranch. He was a boy then, but he remembers a kind woman who lived by herself many miles from town, the Widow Olson.

I also chose to read the poem that night at the Indian Village because I saw Mildred Garrett in the audience. Mildred and her husband, Ed, raised saddle horses, cattle and sheep on the West Side of Goose Lake. They were respected Lake County ranchers and old friends. Ambitious, quiet, kind, the Garretts volunteered their time organizing junior horseshows, donating rodeo livestock, or flipping burgers at the All-Hours Hamburger Stand during Round-Up. They demonstrated their belief in kids, community, rodeo and ranching tradition.

In the early 90s Mildred telephoned to tell us that Ed had died. I suppose I thought that after the funeral she would settle into her role as grandmother and great-grandmother and let the ranch pass into the hands of the next generations. I was wrong. Mildred organized, designed, and promoted a memorial building in Ed's honor to house the history of rodeo in Lake County. She didn't sell out or down. She bought two more ranches and more cattle.

I do not mean to diminish the tragedy of Ed's death or the commitment of their fifty year marriage when I say that the woman I saw that night in 1994 was a new woman, strong and vibrant.

She nodded her head as I read the poem about an independent ranch woman. It was clear that Mildred Garrett and the Widow Olson were one.

# The Widow Olson

So we pass this neat little ranch
on the edge of Catlow Valley.
A perfect community of outbuildings
held apart by government issue poplars and cottonwoods.

"Whose place is that?"
I ask the old buckaroo beside me.

He thinks back to a winter ride
when a teenage wrangle boy drove a herd of horses
one hundred blue miles
measuring each day by the homestead trees in the distance.

"The Widow Olson lives there.
At least she used to.
Her husband died
and she ran the place after that."

His eyes of half Chinese,
half Paiute,
inscrutable to the second power
looks into mine.
I imagine a single woman
120 miles from town,
a day's ride from the nearest neighbor,
riding, working, living
alone.

"How long did she run the place
alone?"

"Oh," he thinks back to her kitchen,
the food on his plate,
the stove by his bed glowing red,
her soaking up the silence of the boy,

"30 or 40 years."

"A woman ran a ranch out here for
30 or 40 years
ALONE
and you still call her
the WIDOW Olson?

What was her first name, Jimmy?"

He thinks along for two jackrabbits,
and a half dozen chuckholes.
"I d'know. We just called her
the Widow Olson."

Then he told me about the next ranch
a day's ride ahead.

*The following poem, "Nevada", was written after I overheard a tourist talking about crossing "the most desolate state in the union." He went on to say that the entire state — except for "Vegas" — ought to be surgically removed, cut out of the country, like cancer. He said that it was, "a nothing state." I wasn't shocked. I had heard it before.*

I imagined his kind setting out on Interstate 80, eastward bound, toward "civilization", slipping a books-on-tape into the player (something like *War and Peace*) and not looking up until they hit the Wasatch. I dedicate this poem to all those souls bereft of understanding — less is more.

# NEVADA

This Nevada land
      is nothing —

      barren
      nothingness of desert
      only colors
      first and last

This raised lava flow
      fierce, ripped, writhing in place
      dusted with millions of years
      layer and layer of wind-blown, rain-carried, pulverized rock
      not even soil
      mere infinitesimal bits sifted up
      and on this
      aspen where snows bank
      quivering as a sage grouse drumming

      is nothing.

Knobs and lines of distant hills
      ink dipped shading pale
      each form — in its own perfection
      within my sight

      nothing.

Breaks,
      short draws draining toward the Yellow Hills
      where stone-hard bones of Lahontan's fish
      Africa's elephant
      Arabia's camel
      Asia's redwood splintered on the sand —

      are nothing.

Shard litter of weapons
        broken stone tools
        around me where I am seated in the enormity of this place
        Earth's heat warming me
        that warmed others forgotten years gone
        bewildered ones who found themselves born here
        roamed, camped, killed, birthed
        starved, sorrowed
        found God, rejoiced God

        all these nothing.

Piddling spring
        that springs
        from the gravel bed
        beneath a rock face raising to a raven's nest
        flows — has always flowed — for miles — more
        knowing least resistance
        sustaining, sustaining

        nothing.

That raven
        glistening black graceless bird
        flapping straight away
        watches time unfold

        and it is nothing.

Shy creatures
        feed, fly
        scuttle, scare
        slither, slip
        haltingly step, arrogantly march
        thunder with conspicuous speed

        nothing.

Sky in brightness
      opalized unearthly colors
      haughty, tauntingly stingy
      a fearsome boiling cauldron
      benevolent
      shadowed, calm
      translucent
      and in that great hollowness of night
      it becomes roan with stars
      expanding to source or destiny?


Silence
      the unshakable
      pierce of silence

      all nothing.

## THE AUTHOR

Linda Hussa is a poet, writer, and rancher living in Cedarville, California. She is the author of *Diary of a Cow Camp Cook, Where the Wind Lives, Ride the Silence,* and *Lige Langston: Sweet Iron.*

## Colophon

Designed by Robert E. Blesse at the Black Rock Press, University of Nevada, Reno Library. The typeface is CalifornianFB, a digital version of Frederick Goudy's University of California Old Style, digitized by Font Bureau's David Berlow—it is also found in another digitized version called Berkeley Old Style. Printed and bound by Thomson Shore, Inc., Dexter, Michigan. Special thanks to Maggie Eirenschmalz who assisted with the production of this book and to Santa Barbara artist Michael Drury who let us use his beautiful oil painting for the cover illustration.